Guide to Apraxia of Speech

Art of Special Needs Parenting™ Series

Stephanie Buckwalter

Dedication

To my husband, Kurt, who has traveled this road with me no matter how lost we became before finding direction again, and still loves me. You are a tower of strength.

To my daughter with apraxia of speech, whose joy of life brings joy to being a special needs parent.

HOW TO USE THIS BOOK

This is a reference book. I used a question and answer format so you don't have to read straight through it. Instead, jump to the answers you really need. If a question references something else in the book, you can follow the link to that page. If I mention a resource, I typically give you a link to where it resides on the internet.

I'll give you fair warning, if you try to read this book straight through you are likely to fall over in boredom. Skip around or read one section at a time to prevent information overload. I alternate using he and she throughout the questions but answers apply equally to both.

ABOUT THE ART OF SPECIAL NEEDS PARENTING SERIES

The *Art of Special Needs Parenting*™ books provide a concise overview of various topics important to special needs families. They are not exhaustive resources on the issues but rather a lifeline in times of stress. They are designed to get you up and running in a short period of time and to answer questions you don't even know to ask. These answers represent hours of research and over two decades of experience.

Contents

Section 1

About Apraxia of Speech

Having apraxia of speech is a lot like visiting a foreign country where you can't speak the language. You may be able to get by with pointing and gesturing, but what if you want to ask about something that is not in the immediate vicinity? Imagine the frustration of trying to get answers to questions like, "How do I get to Munich?" or "Where is the store that sells toner cartridges?"

Further, you can observe what's going on and make intelligent assumptions about what you see, but you don't have the language to ask questions about the things you don't understand. Think about how confusing the world would be if you couldn't ask questions about the things you don't understand like, "What is that weird sound I hear every few hours?" or "Why does the waiter refuse to bring out coffee with my dessert, insisting on treating it as a separate course of the meal?"

And what about the people on the receiving end of your attempts? Most people either can't understand you or don't take the time to try. So, you go about your day doing the best you can with the knowledge and abilities you have, waiting for someone to come along to help you function better in that country. If you are reading this, I assume you are the person someone with apraxia of speech is waiting for. Consider this your guide book.

1

What is apraxia?

Apraxia is a neurological condition that functions like this:

1. A person receives a command or wants to perform an action.
2. The brain sends a signal to the body to perform the action.
3. The body is not able to perform the motor planning to create the action.

When applied to speaking, the condition is called Apraxia of Speech. Apraxia of speech is a neurological disorder that affects the brain's ability to communicate instructions to the mouth and tongue to form speech. When Apraxia of Speech is diagnosed in childhood, it is called Childhood Apraxia of Speech (CAS). This book refers primarily to CAS regarding early intervention and therapy, but provides other information that applies to family life, school and speech therapy throughout childhood into adulthood.

Childhood Apraxia of Speech has been known by other names in the past such as Developmental Apraxia of Speech and Developmental Verbal Dyspraxia. Technically, the term "developmental" means the child could possibly grow out of the condition so that designation has been dropped. The American Speech-Hearing Association (ASHA) uses the term Childhood Apraxia of Speech to encompass both developmental and acquired speech problems, and recognizes that elements of CAS can remain after the normal developmental period. This book uses the terms CAS, apraxia and apraxia of speech interchangeably.

What CAS is not:
- CAS is not a developmental delay of speech. Developmental delay of speech means the child develops speech normally, but at a slower pace.
- CAS is not an intellectual disability. This is an important distinction because in many cultures, the ability to speak is equated with intellect. Typically, a person with CAS can understand far more than they can express with their words or through testing. With CAS, assume intellectual ability.

2

How do I know if my child has apraxia of speech?

As a parent, look for clues such as:

- Feeding difficulties—swallowing problems that can show up as early as nursing or bottle feeding, or you may not notice until solid foods are introduced
- Does not turn toward sounds, showing a lack of awareness of sound
- Reduced cooing or babbling as a baby
- Does not try to imitate sounds
- Delay of the normal time of speech development for individual sounds (Clinical opinion varies on when each sound develops. The list below is only a guide.)
    - Early sounds (18 months to 3 years): p, m, h, w, b
    - Middle sounds (2 to 6 years) d, t, k, g, ng, f, y
    - Later sounds (3 to 8 years) r, l, s, z, j, v, ch, sh, th, zh
- Delay using words, beyond the normal time of speech development
- Reliance on gestures without vocalizations
- Words are not enunciated clearly within appropriate age guidelines
- Ability to speak easily seems to come and go

- Issues with motor planning and sequencing in other, non-speech areas
- People start to comment on your child's speech or lack of it
- A medical professional mentions it or asks questions related to speech showing they might have a concern

A variety of health professionals will often recognize the signs of CAS, but a Speech Language Pathologist (SLP) is the person with the appropriate training to diagnose CAS. If a doctor asks questions about your child's language or mentions apraxia of speech, ask for a referral to an SLP for further evaluation. (*Section 3 Diagnosis and Treatment*)

3

What do I do if I suspect my child has apraxia of speech?

If your child has the speech problems listed above in question 2 or any other communication-related struggles, have your child evaluated by a Speech-Language Pathologist (SLP). They have extensive training in identifying speech issues and can distinguish between apraxia and other speech-language disorders. SLPs are discussed in full detail in *Section 3 Diagnosis and Treatment.*

4

Will my child ever talk?

The answer can be yes, no or maybe. In some cases, a child with CAS learns to speak with a few years of speech therapy. For others, it can take many years of therapy. And with others, speech may not develop beyond a few words or sounds. In cases of pure CAS, meaning no other complications or diagnoses, then appropriate speech therapy can make a lot of difference.

When there are other diagnoses or problems present with CAS, that can complicate matters. Think of a child's interaction with their environment like this:

1. **Body receives input** through the five senses (taste, touch, smell, sound, sight) plus vestibular sense (balance) and proprioceptive sense (where the body is in space)
2. **Brain processes the input** and directs movement or stores information for later use
3. **Body produces motor output** such as walking, talking, hitting a ball, handwriting

With CAS, the problem takes place between steps 2 and 3. The brain gives the body the signal to speak, but the body does not carry out the action properly. Speech therapy primarily focuses on motor output.

5

How long will it take before my child starts to talk?

Each case is different so this question is impossible to answer. There are so many variables in a single case that it is hard to tell. After an evaluation, the Speech-Language Pathologist (see question 14) will recommend a regimen of therapy. With CAS, therapy can last for years but don't be discouraged. The ultimate prize is communication—whether it takes two weeks, two years or ten years.

If your child's future seems kind of fuzzy at this point, keep the long view in mind. Think of these three life stages as they apply to acquiring speech:
- Stage 1: learning to communicate wants and needs (early years)
- Stage 2: getting an education and learning life skills (school age)
- Stage 3: independence in adulthood (beyond high school)

Apraxia will add a layer of challenge to each stage, but it does not determine the outcome. The ability to speak may guide the end results, but by no means is late talking an indication of limitations in adulthood. Keep communication as your focus and work towards it in all areas of life: home, school and community

.

6

What if my child never learns to talk?

It is true that some children may not learn to talk, or may not develop more than functional speech to indicate their basic wants, needs and thoughts. For these children, at some point the question changes to, "Will my child ever be able to communicate?"

Human beings are amazing communicators. They use words, sounds, facial expressions, gesturing and body language. Children with CAS typically have a strong desire to communicate, even if they cannot indicate that with normal speech or with their body movements. They will use whatever abilities they do have to make their needs and wants known.

Be aware that communication can take the form of negative or odd behaviors. For insight into why that happens, read the autobiographies of Ido Kedar (*Ido in Autismland*) and Naoki Higashida, (*The Reason I Jump: The Inner Voice of a Thirteen-Year-Old Boy with Autism*). These teenagers from different cultures wrote about what it is like to be trapped in a body with an active thought life and little ability to communicate, while the people around them try desperately to understand. By using an alternative means to communicate, they were able to dictate their books and share their stories with the world.

Two alternate forms of communication for those with CAS are:
- Sign language

- An augmentative and alternative communication (AAC) device

Sign Language

Sign language uses hand movements, facial expressions and other body movements to communicate. Since apraxia involves problems with motor planning, your child may only be able to approximate the signs. This is fine as long as the communication partner understands what is being said. Teaching young children to sign can be a big relief to them as they learn the means to communicate basic needs without frustration. I recommend the *Signing Time®* series by Rachel Coleman to get started using signs.

As the child begins to interact with more people, sign language is not always practical. Most people do not know sign language. The problem is compounded if the signs are only approximations of the signs instead of the actual signs. Even people who know sign language may not be able to interpret your child's approximations.

American Sign Language (ASL) is its own language with grammar rules that are different than spoken English. The words are presented in a different order than English and smaller words are left out. Signing Exact English (SEE) is another option that teaches one sign per word and uses the same word order as spoken English. Many of the signs are duplicates, but others are not.

AAC

Another option for communication is augmentative and alternative communication (AAC). AAC encompasses methods and solutions that supplement speech (augmentative communication) or replace speech (alternative communication). AAC can be:

- No tech (such as paper and pencil, sign language would also fall into this category)
- Low tech (such as communication binders or boards with pictures, symbols, words or sentences)
- High tech (such as electronic devices with software and speech output)

AAC devices can be as simple as a binder with pictures and symbols or as complex as an iPad with communication software or a dedicated communication device purchased from specialized companies.

A speech therapist trained in AAC can help you decide what device is right for your child. All communication options require some degree of motor planning so if your child struggles with that, you can adapt his communication method to his abilities. You may also find that you start with no tech and then move up to low tech and high tech over time.

Purchasing a dedicated AAC device is an expensive proposition (often thousands of dollars) and you are tied into that company's communication software. This may be ideal in some circumstances, but you can also consider purchasing a tablet and communication software based on your SLP's recommendation.

Some children prefer an iPad because it blends in with their peers' devices but others do better with the bulkier, dedicated communication devices. An added benefit of the dedicated device is that insurance will pay for it as durable medical equipment but they will not always pay for an iPad or the AAC software.

Section 2

Family Life

To paraphrase Charles Dickens, "It is the best of times. It is the worst of times." As a special needs parent, you live that dual reality daily—sometimes moment by moment. There are times of joy punctuated with dips of grief, which make the occasion bittersweet. And there are times of grief punctuated with spikes of joy, which provide hope to keep going. I like to think of it as riding a roller coaster while reading a mystery novel. You not only have the ups and downs of the roller coaster; you also have the suspense of not knowing how things will turn out.

So, what is a parent to do? The first thing is to simply love your child—moment by moment. The next thing is to treat him with dignity and respect, keeping in mind that you hold the upper hand in any verbal exchange. All communication takes work and apraxia compounds the amount of effort it takes. This section provides clues to problems you and your family may face, as well as the good things that come from living with someone with apraxia.

7

What is the biggest problem families face having a child with apraxia of speech?

The biggest problem will likely be the frustration of not knowing what is going on in your child's mind.

- In the early years, this is not as big of a problem because his needs and wants are fairly basic and relate to things that can be identified in the immediate environment. Pointing at an object is sufficient.
- As your child gets older and begins to develop the ability to think with more complexity, he will want to discuss things that can't be pointed to in the immediate area. It takes a lot of work—most of it guesswork— for both parent and child to communicate when that time comes.
- Each time your child's intellect expands but not his ability to communicate, you will see great frustration. He may get angry and act out or suddenly refuse to communicate. You may have to revert back to earlier forms of communication for a while before moving forward again.

Understand that your child's frustration is most likely equal to or greater than yours.

If he will let you, use physical touch to communicate. Sitting beside your child on the couch may be enough to communicate with him. Here are some ideas for activities:

- Read books together, sharing language through associating words with pictures and tone of voice
- Play iPad apps together, or watch your child play with an iPad and comment on the game as he plays
- Bring your phone, laptop or work papers so you are together even if interacting directly is not going well

8

Does having a child with apraxia change the way I parent my child?

In one sense, no. Your values and principles will still be transferred to your child through your daily interactions, regardless of communication style or barriers. In another sense, yes. If your child is misbehaving, you will want to discern the likely cause:

- **Willful defiance** – purposefully going against your instruction (yes, even special needs kids do this)
- **Frustration at not being able to communicate** – frustrated at not having the ability to discuss the instruction by asking questions or negotiating the terms of carrying it out
- **Inability to self-modulate** - when she wants to follow your instruction but her brain will not cooperate, as described in the answer to question 1
- **Having pain or sensory issues** that she doesn't know how to express; when there is a sudden change in behavior from compliance to defiance, this may be the cause

With neuro-typical kids, it is usually fairly straightforward. They are either following your instruction or defying you. With neuro-compromised kids, it may take some work to distinguish between defiance and other issues. This is something you learn as you go.

Once you have identified an act of defiance, then you have to decide how to treat each instance according to your beliefs about parenting. Be careful not to let communication issues become a point of control for either of you.

- On the one hand, be mindful that your instruction is a one-way street, meaning that your child cannot reason with you, ask questions or negotiate for a variation of what you asked for.
- On the other hand, your child might use her inability to communicate to challenge you, testing your authority or even probing your love.

Even if you determine the behavior is not defiance, it may still require correction. Anything you can do to correct behavior toward socially acceptable norms will go a long way toward acceptance for your child, both with peers and in public—regardless of root cause of the behavior.

9

What problems are typical for a child with apraxia?

The physical problems are:
- Challenges with speech production
- Motor planning, which may also be seen in areas other than speech
- Difficulty swallowing food

You may also see some or all of the following:
- Lots of frustration due to
  - Not being able to communicate what they are thinking
  - Not being able to ask questions
  - Not being able to negotiate a request
  - Not knowing what to ask
  - Not understanding the world around them (their world often does not make sense to them unless someone explains it)
- Resistance to therapy because it's hard work
- Problems with self-modulation due to sensory issues, especially when apraxia is only part of a child's diagnosis

As they get older and more aware, they may deeply feel the effects of:

- Rejection
- Knowing they are different

- Being made fun of
- Not being able to keep up with a conversation because they can't form words fast enough or follow the conversation while trying to form words
- Being talked about while they are standing right there and can't add to the conversation or defend themselves

As your child becomes self-aware and starts to notice how others respond, keep a look out for signs of depression or sadness. Talk to your child about what is going on and give them a way to tell you how they are feeling, through words, signs or using AAC.

10

What problems are typical of the parents? Mom? Dad?

Both parents should have a basic understanding of the diagnosis and what that means for the child. The parent who goes to the bulk of the doctor appointments (usually mom) may have an unequal understanding of the reality and challenges; therefore, it may be tough to make decisions that you agree on.

Both parents will go through a grieving process. When you have a child with a disability, there is always a sense of loss—usually over and over again. You probably had dreams about yourself as a parent, and what your child would be like and all the things they would accomplish. When circumstances alter those dreams, the sense of loss can be deep, and surprising. It is okay to grieve, but don't get stuck there.

Even though your child may not fit into those early dreams, you can—and should— build new dreams. They may be bittersweet, but your child only knows what her life is like now, not what dreams you had in the past. Although it may be hard at first, dream big for your child's future. Every life is significant.

Moms often carry the emotional burden of having a child who is different. In a negative way, this can manifest as rejection, shame, guilt or jealousy. On the positive side, strong emotions provide motivation to search for answers, to work through the problems and for the hours of therapy needed to move forward. Moms need a healthy outlook and coping skills to keep from being consumed by their emotions.

Dads more typically feel the weight of responsibility for the child's future. Their concern is for relationships (roommates, marriage) and being provided for (job, trust fund). These concerns may not apply to an apraxia-of-speech-only diagnosis, but they can still be a concern.

Both mom and dad need coping mechanisms to learn how to
- Deal with negative emotions
- Grieve the very real losses
- Appreciate the child as he or she is at this moment
- Stay motivated to help their child
- Reach out to others for help and support

You may find that you and your spouse fall into coping mechanisms you had when you were single. At that time, you were alone or relied on other people. You may have to relearn how to cope by leaning on your spouse, which can take some work. Coping together is better than coping alone side-by-side.

11

How does CAS affect siblings?

Having a child with special needs affects the whole family. The family dynamics change when one child needs more of the parent's attention than the others. As you read through this list, look for subjects you might need to talk about with your other kids.

- Siblings have to work harder to communicate, just like mom and dad.
- They too experience the pain of rejection as others tend to avoid people who are different.
- At certain ages, they have to deal with embarrassment around peers, especially if their sibling communicates in inappropriate ways like grunting, lashing out or yelling.
- Siblings may feel like their problems are comparatively minor so their issues are not worth their parents' time.
- They may be unable to express how they really feel about their sibling for fear of offending their parents or because they feel guilty about how they feel.
- Siblings may have a hard time switching to normal communication with peers.
- They may have a heightened sensitivity to parents' relational struggles or underlying stress.

On the positive side:
- Siblings often develop compassion for those who are different.
- They tend to be more responsible due to helping out with their sibling.
- They learn alternate ways to communicate.
- They tend to think about life with a more sober outlook.

The key to resolving most of these issues is open communication. Topics may need to be covered more than once over the years depending on age and circumstances. You may need to explain a diagnosis one way at age three and another way at age ten. Here are a few ideas for addressing some common issues as they occur:
- Talk about their sibling's problems, and how they can explain it to others.
- Show that it is okay to be frustrated about their sibling, and teach them coping mechanisms.
- Explain that their sibling may take more of your time, but not more of your love.
- Assure them that their problems are just as important as their sibling's problems, and make time to listen to their struggles, offer support and follow up with their needs
- Discuss the reality that you will need their help from time to time, but to let you know if they feel it is too much for them (just as it often feels like it is too much for you)
- Let them know that even though you may argue with your spouse, you are trying to work things out for everyone in the family.
- Encourage them to do things with neuro-typical kids and not feel guilty about what they can do that their sibling can't.

12

Where can I find support for apraxia of speech?

When your child has special needs, you can't realistically go it alone. You will most likely have a team of people who help you get what your child needs including:

- doctors
- therapists
- care givers
- teachers
- aides (for some diagnoses)

- family members
- friends

- support groups
- support organizations

The first group are people who are paid to help your child. You are paying them to give you advice, services and support. In the early days, you will rely heavily on what they advise or recommend. That is a good thing. As your child grows and you learn more about apraxia and how it affects your child specifically, you will be able to ask better questions and find help specific to your child.

Family and friends, if they are willing, can contribute child care, emotional support and practical help. It also helps to have at least one friend outside of your family that you can rely on unconditionally, whether to call to complain, ask for help or simply get you out of the house for a while. Friends and family may react by pulling away. It may be that they just don't know how to respond to your child or your struggles. Teach them how to communicate with you child. Talk about what your child likes to do and what abilities they do have so they know how to interact with your child. You already know how hard it is to communicate with your child so help them out.

A word of warning to help set your expectations: your church or religious organization may not be set up to handle a special needs child. Often, we'd like to think we can turn there for help and support but the painful reality is that it's not always the case. You may find yourself advocating for your child at church as much as you do at school or in the community. Again, talk about what your child likes to do and what abilities they do have so others know how to interact with your child.

Support groups can help you find people who identify with your problems. Most support groups are organized around either diagnosis or type of therapy. To find a group, enter your child's diagnosis or type of therapy plus the word group in a search engine, such as apraxia group or autism group. Add the word local if you are looking for local groups that meet in person. You can also use those same terms searching in:

- Facebook groups
- Yahoo groups
- Meetups
- Forums
- Blogs

I recommend three starting points for support organizations. The first two are specific to apraxia of speech and will give you solid information and research about the diagnosis. The third one covers special needs related to intellectual and developmental disabilities and helps you locate people who can help you maneuver the complex world of disability.

- ASHA.org. The main professional organization for apraxia of speech is the American Speech-Language-Hearing Association (ASHA). Their website covers the issues extensively in all areas: legal, insurance, best practices, research, advocacy and more.

- Apraxia-Kids.org. A nonprofit organization committed to educating parents and professionals and raise awareness in the community. They offer articles, webinars and a national conference, among other things.

- TheARC.org. The ARC operates through chapters, some local, some regional, some state, as well as at the national level. They advocate for people with disabilities across multiple areas such as legislation, education, medical (including Medicaid waivers), recreation, employment, living accommodations, family support, long-term planning and more. They work with people of all ages, not just children.

Section 3

Diagnosis and Treatment

The best news in this book is that there are solutions to the problems presented by apraxia of speech. Speech therapy will be your first order of treatment. Some kids recover completely from apraxia of speech. But even for those who fall somewhere along the spectrum of profound-severe-moderate-mild-resolving-resolved, there is hope. Thankfully, we live in a time where brain research and technology, among other things, have provided advances in helping those with apraxia to communicate in other ways.

This section addresses how apraxia of speech is diagnosed and treated through the services of a Speech-Language Pathologist (SLP). Speech therapy directly addresses the problem of apraxia of speech. The success of speech therapy varies depending on each individual case. When there are multiple diagnoses, you have to take into consideration the nature and severity of each diagnosis in the child's complete medical picture.

13

How is apraxia of speech diagnosed?

Diagnosis includes a comprehensive evaluation by a Speech-Language Pathologist (SLP) and may include information from other medical professionals as well. The SLP will look at areas such as:

- Sound inventory, noting the number of sounds, syllables and words your child can produce
- Airflow, to see if it is sufficient to produce sounds
- The interior of the mouth, for shape and function related to speech and swallowing
- Intonation and volume of speech
- Intelligibility of words, including sequencing of sounds and sound combinations
- Complexity of speech, including consistency and accuracy
- Communicative intent, even if the child has no speech
- Oral-motor skills, or how the mouth functions during different tasks
- Hearing screening, to make sure the child is hearing what is spoken

Using this evaluation and your child's medical history, the SLP will give a "differential diagnosis," meaning that the results fit within a specific speech or language disorder. The diagnosis may include the severity of the disorder and the recommended treatment, among other things.

Sometimes the assessment is not definitive and instead, the diagnosis comes as the result of observation over the course of treatment.

14

What is a Speech-Language Pathologist (SLP) and what do they do?

A Speech-Language Pathologist (SLPs) is the medical professional with the appropriate training to diagnose and treat problems with speech, language and swallowing. They evaluate and treat most problems related to speech and language.

Speech is the how to of getting the words out. Speech disorders affect things like: articulation (sounds), phonology (speech patterns), apraxia (planning and coordinating speech), fluency (stuttering) and voice (if vocalizations are hoarse).

Language deals with comprehension of speech. Language disorders cover things like receptive language (understanding), expressive language (using) and pragmatic language (appropriate use in social situations). Comprehension of language has implications for overall communication ability, not just speaking ability.

Other disorders that SLPs address include deafness/hearing loss (through lip reading, speech production, AAC), oral-motor problems (muscles that don't work) and swallowing/feeding disorders (which use the same muscles as speech).

An SLP may refer a client to other therapists or doctors to address problems that affect speech such as a physical therapist or a neurologist. For example, hearing and auditory processing play a part in speech, but those problems are diagnosed by an audiologist.

Please note that even though an SLP is the correct professional to diagnose apraxia of speech, your insurance may require the diagnosis to come from a medical doctor (M.D.). Your SLP can refer your child to a doctor or neurologist for a letter of medical necessity with the appropriate diagnosis code.

Treatment

In addition to evaluating and diagnosing speech, language and swallowing disorders, SLPs can also treat these disorders. They can work with both children and adults, but some may choose to specialize by
- Age (pediatric, elder care)
- Developmental (born with apraxia) versus acquired (stroke, brain injury)
- Some other differentiator (hearing impaired, AAC)

SLPs work in a variety of settings including:
- Schools
- Private clinics
- Hospitals
- Nursing homes
- Public health agencies
- Universities
- State and federal government agencies
- Health departments

- Research laboratories

With a diagnosis of CAS, it is most likely that long-term therapy will be received through private clinics or the school system. However, there are programs in each state that you may qualify for that will open up other avenues to speech therapy. Some of the deciding factors for how and where your child receives therapy are the state you live in, your insurance coverage and severity of the problem. Some of these programs are discussed in *Section 5 Educational Considerations*.

15

What do I do if I suspect my child has speech problems?

Sometimes it is difficult to distinguish between speech problems and delayed speech. With delayed speech, speech develops normally but the timeline is delayed. If speech patterns are not normal or speech is delayed outside the norms, your child could have speech problems that need more attention.

There are several routes to identifying speech issues and the need for therapy, depending on your child's age:

- If your child is young (under 3 years old), your first stop would be your pediatrician. You can ask the doctor about your child's speech. They may refer you to a speech-language pathologist (SLP) for an evaluation or to a program available in your state for Early Intervention. Early Intervention is mandated by IDEA, the law governing schools and children with disabilities (explained in *Section 5 Educational Considerations*).
- In some states, you can contact the Early Intervention services office directly. In others, you have to be referred by a doctor. The exact name may vary from state to state, but if you search on early intervention and your state's name, you should be able to find a program for infants and toddlers.

- Once your child is 3 years old, they no longer qualify for Early Intervention, but then you have access to the Child Find program in your state, which is also mandated by IDEA, the law governing schools and children with disabilities. It requires school districts to find all children who have disabilities and need services. Services offered are related to preparing them to succeed in school now and adult life later. This would include speech services for children with CAS and other diagnoses (more in *Section 5 Educational Considerations*).

- If your child is already in school, a teacher at school may notice problems and recommend an evaluation through the school. You also can request an evaluation from the school, a right granted in IDEA.

- Another option is to contact an SLP directly and set up an evaluation. Read your policy or call your insurance company before taking this step. The initial evaluation will likely be covered by insurance, but not always. It may only be covered if referred by your primary care physician or other doctor. Regular therapy appointments may or may not be covered. (See *Section 4 Insurance* for more details.) Before proceeding to the evaluation, be certain you know what your insurance will cover and get all the paperwork in place before you go.

16

Is it important to get a formal diagnosis?

Yes. Even though receiving a diagnosis for your child can be painful or you may not agree with it, that label has several benefits:

- It provides a common language for you to speak to others about your child, especially health and educational professionals and related organizations.
- It opens the door to early intervention and educational services.
- The associated diagnostic code(s) provide evidence to insurance companies for payment toward therapy and related services.
- It opens the door to other services in the community.

17

When should my child start therapy?

The quick answer is: as soon as you know there is a problem. CAS is difficult to officially diagnose because you have to wait until the child demonstrates problems with speech or the normal window for speech development has passed and the child is not producing appropriate sounds or words. Even if the official diagnosis comes later, you can start therapy long before that with a diagnosis of potential speech problems. Waiting for speech to develop or the window for normal speech development to pass will cost you valuable time. With CAS, the child needs help getting the brain to communicate with the mouth so the earlier you start that process, the better the potential outcome. Speech therapy is a necessary part of treatment for apraxia of speech.

18

Should I ask my doctor to test for other problems?

Childhood Apraxia of Speech often occurs alongside other medical issues. If you notice any symptoms that fall outside the norm or give you cause for concern, it is best to have them checked out. Your doctor may or may not be able to diagnose your child's problem but should be able to refer you to a medical professional who can.

When it comes to getting medical help for your child, it's always best to have concrete data—especially when dealing with multiple doctors and therapists across many specialties. Keep copies of all test results, evaluations and other medical data for your child in a binder that you take to all doctor appointments. Every bit of data is a clue to how to best help your child. Concrete data is especially helpful in cases with apraxia since the patient won't necessarily have the ability to speak for themselves and indicate areas of struggle, pain or preferences.

19

Is there anything else I can do besides speech therapy?

Speech therapy is your first stop in getting help and the main remedy for speech disorders, including apraxia of speech. However, there are other therapies people have found helpful, especially when there are multiple diagnoses. These therapies do not directly work on the speech mechanism, but support the overall health of the body or target other problems.

Supplemental and alternative therapies vary widely in type and application. They might address:
- Toxins
- Allergens
- Microbes
- Gut imbalances
- Vitamin and mineral deficiencies
- Inflammation
- Emotional health
- Retained reflexes
- Brain imbalances

Choosing any supplemental or alternative therapy should start with an evaluation by a professional to see if your child would benefit. Many people will do research and jump on bandwagon after bandwagon. Spending your money up front on proper evaluations will likely save you thousands of dollars in the long run.

If you are relying on stories you hear around the web, remember that each child's health picture is unique and their cases may have variables not present in your case that would potentially change the outcome. It is far better to get a snapshot of what is going on in your child's body through medical testing so you can evaluate claims and apply therapies from a position of knowledge, not of ignorance.

20

How do I evaluate a therapy to know if it is legitimate?

Evaluating a therapy is complex. It can take a long time to gain an understanding of the facts because it requires knowing:

- The underlaying rationale for the therapy
- Whether the recommendations are evidence based or anecdotal
- How doctors use medical papers and clinical trials
- How a study or clinical trial came about
- Who is paying for the study
- Who is trying to sell you the therapy solution

Each of these items should be considered when evaluating a therapy approach or method.

Section 4

Insurance

Coverage for apraxia of speech is not always a straightforward proposition. Coverage can be hidden in areas not related to speech services so it pays to know where to look. This section will help you understand how coverage for diagnosis and treatment is offered and provide some terms you should know. Knowing this in advance of seeking services will go a long way toward having your claims paid by the insurance company.

When you do have a problem with insurance, it usually boils down to one question: who pays? If you and the insurance company disagree on the answer, then you have to be willing to provide supporting documentation for why you believe they should pay. This section explains how to support your position if you end up in this situation and potential avenues of support.

21

How do I find out what is covered by insurance?

Not all insurance policies cover speech or language services. When they do, finding the section of your policy that relates to speech and language coverage can be tricky. Below are some sections you can look under, depending on how it is worded in your policy.

- Speech therapy
- Speech-language pathology
- Speech pathology
- Rehabilitation services
- Other rehabilitation services
- Other medically necessary services
- Durable medical equipment (for dedicated speech devices)
- Things we don't cover
- Exclusions to coverage
- Charges covered with special limitations

To figure it out exactly, there are three ways you can find out about your coverage:

1. Read your insurance policy. If you received a paper copy or a link to an online service, you can read about your benefits. This is the best place to start so you know what questions to ask if you use one of the next options.

2. Contact the insurance company directly. You can call them, or a lot of insurance companies have websites where you can check what your policy covers and get a list of in-network providers. If you are asking a representative to clarify something you read in your policy, ask them to send it to you in writing. Their interpretation may become an issue if a claim is denied because of what you thought they said. Always write down the name of the person you spoke to, date and time, and how long it will take them to get the written explanation to you. Take notes on the conversation so you can see if your version matches their written interpretation.

3. Contact the Human Resources (HR) department of the company issuing the policy. They usually have someone who specializes in benefits. They can explain everything to you and can contact the insurance company on your behalf if they need clarification for your situation.

22

Are there any terms I should know related to insurance?

Navigating the world of insurance is no small task. Here are some terms that will be helpful as you begin your journey:

- **ICD codes/billing codes** –ICD stands for International Classification of Diseases. As of this writing, the current ICD manual is ICD-10. The ICD diagnosis classification system was developed by the Centers for Disease Control and Prevention for use in all U.S. health care treatment settings. In addition to diseases, the codes can designate injuries, symptoms, abnormal findings and other diagnoses. Insurance companies use these codes, provided by medical care givers on claims forms, to pay for claims. Be sure your SLP uses the proper code for a diagnosis of apraxia and not the one for a general speech delay. Apraxia is a speech disorder and is more likely to be covered by insurance.

- **habilitative versus rehabilitative care** –Most insurance companies cover rehabilitative care—getting back function, such as speech, that was lost due to injury such as occurrences of stroke or brain injury. They do not always cover habilitative care—helping the child to gain functions they never developed, such as speech. When your child is born with apraxia of speech, therapy is regarded as habilitative. During your child's early years, there are government mandated programs that will help you with speech therapy but once your child reaches school age, those programs end. The school will evaluate your child for speech services, but those will be related to educational needs. If your child *clinically* requires more speech therapy than the school offers *educationally*, you may be able to get speech therapy through sections of your insurance policy that cover habilitative services, but expect a long, drawn-out process if it is not explicitly stated in your policy. Some states have passed laws requiring insurance companies to provide habilitative care.

- **durable medical equipment** –qualifying Augmentative and Assistive Communication (AAC) devices fall under this part of your insurance policy
- **case manager** – point of contact at the insurance company to manage complex cases (see question 26)
- **explanation of benefits (EOB)** – a letter you receive for each claim submitted. It is financial documentation of who pays each portion of a claim. Check these against the final bill that comes in from the provider to make sure the numbers match.
- **medical necessity** – Medical necessity generally means that treatment is considered reasonable, necessary, and/or appropriate, based on evidence-based clinical standards of care.
- **prior authorization** – Some insurance policies require you to get authorization for services from the insurance company before you see a specialist or therapist. This is not the same thing as a referral, which originates from a doctor.

While we're on the topic of prior authorization, be aware that the insurance company may also require prior authorization for urgent care and emergency room visits. If your child has feeding or swallowing problems related to speech or has health issues that might require emergency care, it is a good idea to look up these requirements in advance so you know the procedure. During a medical emergency, if you don't already know what to do, seek immediate care and then call your insurance company as soon as you can.

23

What do I look for in the insurance policy?

Your policy may cover some or all of the following:

- **Speech evaluation**—some insurance companies may require
  - A referral from a doctor
  - Pre-authorization or pre-certification by the insurance company BEFORE the appointment takes place
- **Speech therapy**—but may be limited by
  - Total number of sessions or hours per year
  - Total dollar amount per year
  - Total number of sessions or hours per life of the policy
  - Reason for therapy (swallowing issues can be life threatening so therapy may be covered as a medical necessity but not for speech production)
- **Durable medical equipment**
  - Dedicated AAC devices are considered medical devices.
  - This does not automatically include an iPad with AAC software, but you can try to work with your insurance company to cover the cost.

Note that some insurance companies may pay for an evaluation but not for speech therapy. Paperwork can take a long time so get started on it immediately upon referral for an evaluation. The initial appointment for an evaluation is more expensive than regular sessions. They should last longer and include a full report on findings. Be sure to get a copy of this report as it will be the baseline for measuring progress.

24

How do I appeal to the insurance company when they refuse a claim?

When starting the process of appealing a claim, document every phone call, email and person spoken to until the claim is resolved. The insurance company documents everything on their end, but it is their version of events. You need to keep your own record of events and document the name of the person you spoke to for accountability purposes. Note the time and date of the call or email correspondence also.

The first step in your fact-finding mission is to call the insurance company to:

- Ask why the claim was denied (they should have a reason based on the policy).
- Request a written explanation and a copy of the portion of the policy they are basing it on.
- Ask if there is any additional information the insurance company needs in order to process the claim for payment (such as a statement of medical necessity or additional medical records).

Once you have all that information, write a letter to the insurance company requesting the claim be reviewed. You may find yourself educating the claims department on apraxia of speech and why it requires extensive speech therapy.

You will likely need to develop a case, much like a lawyer would in a courtroom, for why the insurance company should pay the claim. Keep records of all letters sent, dates, responses and so on. In your letter to the insurance company:

- Quote your policy
- Quote medical studies, papers and research
- Quote local or state laws applicable to habilitative care

Assume you will have to go through several rounds of appeals to get services covered. Insurance companies often count on the fact that most people will give up after the first denial of a claim. They are a for-profit business and the less they pay out, the more profit they make. Keep that in mind as you begin your appeals process. Sometimes it is only a single piece of information missing that gets a claim rejected. Follow through to get your rightful reimbursements. Keep in mind that if you miss the deadline for filing claims, that will be the end of the matter.

It is a good idea to copy your company's benefits department on the letter. Provide them with everything you sent to the insurance company, plus your documentation of all correspondence and phone calls to date with the insurance company. They can call the insurance company on your behalf if needed.

If you believe you are being unfairly denied coverage or the insurance company is not responsive, you can register a complaint with your state's Department of Insurance.

25

Should I consider an out-of-network provider?

Be careful when using out-of-network doctors or therapists. Some insurance policies have a high deductible (several thousand dollars) before they will even begin paying for out-of-network services. That means you will pay several thousand dollars at the beginning of each plan year before insurance reimbursement kicks in. Then, the deductible is usually higher so that adds more out-of-pocket expenses.

Specialists charge more for appointments. Speech therapy can last for several years. Keep both of these in mind when calculating costs and selecting providers for your child.

26

Are there any secrets I should know about working with the insurance company?

There are some things the insurance company will not necessarily reveal if you do not know the right questions to ask. There is one secret worth knowing if your child has a complex case, sees many doctors and therapists, or if you have reason for continued contact with the insurance company over claims. You can request a case manager. Insurance companies have them but they don't always advertise the fact. Be sure to request one who is familiar with special needs children.

When you are assigned a case manager, you have one point of contact with the insurance company instead of calling the usual number and getting a random contact. A case manager can get referrals approved, help you find in-network doctors and explain certain processes. If you get someone who is hostile to your case, you can try to request another one. Your case manager may be friendly and they may help you in a lot of ways but always remember that, in the end, they work for the insurance company, not you.

27

Are there other ways to get help paying for my child's medical care?

Here are some other avenues to getting help with your child's medical care costs:

- **Insurance riders.** If you have private insurance that does not cover speech issues, you can contact the employer's human resources/benefits department and request they add a rider to the company policy for speech and language services. Expect to educate them about apraxia and how it requires long-term and intensive therapy by providing supporting documents. The more they understand, the better the coverage they add is likely to be. You can request an Employer Insurance packet from ASHA to help you with this process.

- **Other sections of your existing policy.** If your child has multiple diagnoses, those may fall under different parts of your insurance policy that would cover speech therapy such as habilitative care for congenital problems (your child is born with the problem). Habilitative versus rehabilitative care is a current hot topic. Some states have passed legislation requiring coverage for some habilitative care. The autism community is very active in this area, educating and working with state legislatures to pass laws requiring coverage of habilitative care.

- **Medicare waivers.** Medicare waivers are designed to help provide services to certain groups of people, including those with intellectual disabilities, developmental disabilities and autism. Each state administers its own program. You will likely be on a waiting list for years so apply immediately if you want to start receiving funds at some point. Some states have more than one type of waiver so explore all your options. Contact your local ARC (starting at thearc.org) for information on what is available in your state and how to apply for a waiver.
- **University programs.** If you live near a university with a speech-language pathology training program, you may be able to get appointments with SLPs in training at a reduced rate.
- **Secondary health insurance.** If you have secondary insurance, check to see if the policy covers speech and language services or offers other appropriate coverage.
- **Health Savings Accounts** (also called flex spending accounts). HSA money can be applied toward speech therapy. Although this money comes from your own pocket, it is tax free so it offers a little savings.
- **Research studies.** If your child qualifies for a research study that covers speech services, you can apply for the study. Keep in mind that you may have to keep detailed records or go to a specific medical facility for regular appointments.
- **Grants.** You can apply for grants from a variety of organizations for therapy and for assistive communication devices. Search for speech therapy grants.
- **Third parties.** Some organizations offer financial help to families in need of medical care.

28

What kinds of records should I keep?

Eligibility for services and programs depends on your ability to prove certain things about your child. You will need to keep track of paperwork for decades. Even if you do not think you will need the information now, it may be required for services as your child transitions to adult life. Here is a list of things you will want to keep related to speech issues and other medical concerns. In general, keep all records indefinitely or until you are certain your child's diagnosis no longer applies. If in doubt, copy it and keep it.

General Info

- **Contact info for all healthcare professionals**. Full name, name of practice, phone, fax, email, specialty, website.
- **Contact info for pharmacies you use regularly**. Name, address, phone number for pharmacy. Also, nearest 24-hour pharmacy.
- **Copies of insurance cards, front and back**. Keep these for a few years in case you need to provide proof of continuous medical coverage.
- **Allergies**. Keep a list of known allergies to both medicine and food. If your child has reactions to food dyes or aspartame,

note that too. Occasionally, prescriptions include non-pharmaceutical ingredients that may affect your child.

- **Vaccinations**. Keep an up-to-date record of these. Every time your child receives another vaccination, get another print out of the record.
- **Developmental milestones**. You will be asked about these over and over, even into adulthood. They will be helpful for you, too, to track your child's progress over time. For speech, try to keep records on when the following develop:
  - when baby babbles
  - says individual sounds
  - says first words
  - puts two words together
  - uses short sentences

Medical History

- **Test Results**. Keep copies of all test results. It makes life much easier when you can show test results ordered by other doctors during an appointment. If you have access to test results online, print those out and keep them.
- **Assessments**. In addition to assessments for speech, you will also want to keep medical, educational and psychological assessments that identify a diagnosis or need for services. They provide proof of need.
- **Diagnoses.** Anything with a diagnosis on it should be kept, even if you don't agree with the diagnosis or the diagnosis lasted only a short while. Proof of disability will open the doors to services in the areas of medical care, education, government programs, special sports leagues, employment, housing, special needs trusts and

other things you can't imagine today or may not even exist at this time.

- **Medications**. Keep track of all medications, doses, frequency taken, when medication was started, when ended. Some medications interact with others so it is important to share this list with doctors who prescribe new medications for your child. Most intake forms require it so it is best to have it well documented. Before an appointment, you can take a picture of the label for current prescription information.

- **Supplements**. Some supplements interact with or reduce the efficacy of prescription medication so know your supplements and keep a list of these at hand. Most intake forms ask about supplements. You can take a picture of the label before appointments to keep track. If the supplement has more than one ingredient listed, take a picture of the nutrition information box on the label that lists everything in it.

- **Therapies**. Keep track of all therapies, when they started, frequency and when they ended. You will want this information for years to come.

- **Hospitalizations**. Note the dates, reason and outcomes. This information is requested on most intake forms. You will need it for years to come.

Other Records to Keep at Home

- **Insurance policy**. Copy of the portion of the policy that covers speech services or any other part of the policy that applies to your situation.

- **Explanation of Benefits (EOB) Letters**. When the insurance company receives a claim, they will send you an EOB, explaining what they will pay and what you can expect to be billed on each claim from appointments and hospital stays. Keep these and match them with the bills that come from care providers to make sure you are receiving the correct payments. This can be a significant amount of paperwork if you have a lot of appointments. Think of yourself as the benefits department of your home and maintain it accordingly.

- **Approval letters.** Some services base your eligibility on approval from other programs, such as Supplemental Security Income (SSI) or Medicaid. In other words, if you qualify SSI, you would qualify for other programs automatically (jobs training, SNAP aka food stamps). You will need to show the approval letter from one program in order to receive services through another program.
- **Proof of citizenship.** This is not necessarily insurance related, but it can cause problems for your child later in life—especially if something happens to you without this being taken care of. If your child was adopted from a foreign country, be sure you have all this paperwork taken care of at an early age.

Section 5

Educational Considerations

Think of what it would be like to go through your whole school experience and never be able to ask a question, make a comment or give the answer to a question. That would be a miserable experience. Speech is so important that the Individuals with Disabilities Education Act (IDEA) requires that any disability—or sometimes even potential disabilities—be addressed beginning at birth. It specifically mentions speech services so children with apraxia can receive help through programs mandated by IDEA.

This section provides a high-level overview some of the requirements of IDEA and how you can use that to prepare your child for school and beyond. Even if you decide to homeschool or send your child to private school, you may still be able to take advantage of some of the provisions of IDEA, especially in the birth-to-before-Kindergarten years.

29

What is the Individuals with Disabilities Education Act (IDEA) and how does it affect my child?

The Individuals with Disabilities Education Act (IDEA) is a federal education law passed in 1975 that must be reauthorized every five years. Some highlights of the legislation are:

- It covers children from birth through high school, divided into the following stages of your child's education:
    - Early Intervention (birth up to 3 years)
    - Child Find (3 to 5 years)
    - Individualized Education Plan (IEP) (K-12th grade)
    - Transition Services (beginning at age 14)
- It requires schools to provide a free and appropriate public education (FAPE) to every child. Schools provide FAPE through one or more of the following: specialized instruction, related services (like speech therapy), accommodations and assistive technology.
- It gives children with certain learning disabilities special help to access the curriculum. Not all children with learning disabilities will qualify for services. However, "speech or language impairment" is one of thirteen categories of disabilities listed specifically in IDEA.

30

What is Early Intervention (birth to 3 years)?

Early intervention isn't just about getting help for your child at a young age. It is the name of a government program required under the Individuals with Disabilities Education Act (IDEA). Early intervention services provide children with developmental delays or specific health conditions with services to help them catch up to developmental norms. This includes significant delays evident from the start or conditions that are likely to lead to a delay such as hearing loss or birth defects. In addition, some states allow for other criteria. Speech evaluations and therapy are services offered through this program.

- Early intervention covers children from birth to three years old.
- The program operates with federal grants so services are offered for free or at a low cost.
- You do not need a referral for this program.
- You can contact the program office directly for an evaluation.
- Speech services are provided in your home at no cost to you.
- Search on Early Intervention plus your state to find out how to access services.

Since education falls to the state and not the federal government, each state implements the program according to both federal and state laws. Because of this, there may be differences with Early Intervention programs from state to state. The idea behind the law is that early intervention will increase a child's chances of success in education and in life.

31

What is Child Find (3-5 years)?

Once your child reaches age three, the state can decide to extend Early Intervention services or your child may be eligible for regular special education services. These services are provided through the Individuals with Disabilities Education Act (IDEA) in the Child Find mandate. Programs are administered by your local school.

- If your child was in an Early Intervention program, program specialists will most likely help you transition to Child Find services.
- If your child was not in Early Intervention, you can seek Child Find services for your child. According to IDEA, all school districts are required to locate and evaluate all children with disabilities. Search for Child Find in your state to start the process.
- You can use Child Find services even if your child will not attend public school. If you plan to homeschool, pay special attention to how this will affect the paperwork you have to file starting in Kindergarten related to homeschooling. Each state is different.

The Child Find process starts with an evaluation. If your child is identified as one who may need services, your child will be given an evaluation free of charge. School personnel will review the results of all tests given and decide if your child qualifies for any special education services including speech therapy.

32

What if my child still doesn't talk by the time he/she starts school?

First, your child is not alone. Many students still need help with communication when starting school. If not already in process from the programs mentioned above, you can request that your child be evaluated for speech services as part of an Individualized Education Plan (IEP) according to the requirements of the Individuals with Disabilities Education Act (IDEA). (See question 34 for more information on how far in advance you should begin the process.) If it is determined services are needed, your school will supply speech services as part of your child's regular education.

Several things to note here about speech services from this point forward:

- The school does not give anywhere near what you would get if you were to have private speech therapy. Their justification is often that their determination of the amount of time needed for services is educational, not clinical. Prepare for this discussion by researching ASHA's guidelines on your child's specific needs for speech therapy using research-based evidence. Print out all the evidence you are using and present it at the IEP meeting and have it added as part of your child's school record. That way if you ever go to due process, those pieces of evidence will be reviewed as part of your case.

- Your insurance company may not be as willing to cover speech therapy after school age. This may not be true in all cases, but it can be quite a surprise. The reasoning seems to be that by school age, the developmental stage is finished and the school can take over for educational needs. Talk to your insurance company way in advance and be prepared to build a case for your child's need for ongoing therapy using ASHA documents and any legal cases that may apply to your situation.

- Plan to work with your child at home on speech. Hopefully, you have been working with your child's speech therapist throughout this time and learning how to do some of the exercises. You can also ask the school speech therapist to give your child speech homework if you are willing to do it.

33

What is an IEP (K-12ᵗʰ grade) and will my child need one?

An IEP is an Individualized Education Plan. It is a legally binding document that lays out the services and supports your child will receive as the school educates your child while providing a Free and Appropriate Public Education (FAPE). The requirements for what goes into an IEP are laid out in the Individuals with Disabilities Education Act (IDEA) and your state's education laws.

- The first step is an evaluation for each area of need. This is typically done by the school for free.
- Once the evaluations are complete, the parents and school come together to create the student's IEP. An IEP meeting is essentially an administrative meeting where the school documents how they will administer special education law to your child based on discussions between the parents and the school. You have the right to bring people to the meeting to help you develop the IEP. Everyone at the meeting constitutes the team of people who will decide how the law is administered to your child.
- The team will review the evaluations during the meeting to see if the student qualifies for accommodations, additional services or to be in contained classrooms that are tailored to children with special educational needs.
- The end result of an IEP meeting is

- o a plan for educating your child
- o a team of individuals who are tasked with making it happen

An IEP is, at its heart, a legal issue. The best books written about IEPS are those published by Wrights Law. The one about keeping the emotion out of an IEP, *From Emotions to Advocacy: The Special Education Survival Guide*, is probably the best one to start with. It explains the legal requirements and processes, how to make the most of the meetings and how to hold the school accountable for their part. IEP meetings can be a challenge. However, if you understand the process and the role the parent(s) play, it will go a long way toward getting your child the education and services they need.

There is also a document called a 504 plan, named after *Section 504 of the Rehabilitation Act of 1973*. A 504 plan falls under civil rights related to discrimination against people with disabilities. A 504 plan is not part of the special education law, but you can still receive speech services in a general education setting using a 504 plan.

34

Should I consider other schooling options such as homeschool or private school?

In all 50 states of the US, you are free to educate your child in the best way you see fit. You can choose public, private, charter or homeschool. If you are looking for help related to speech, here are some things you will want to consider:

Charter Schools

- A charter school is a public school so your child will receive an IEP, which will include speech services if your child qualifies.

Private Schools

- Private schools do not typically offer IEPs but you can have your child evaluated through the public school system for services. However, even though IDEA requires that public schools find and evaluate children, they are not required to provide services to children outside the public school system. One reason is because IDEA and state laws list requirements for teachers of special education that private school teachers may not meet.

- Some school districts offer a service plan which is similar to an IEP but offers less. Other states offer no support to students in private schools
- Some private schools are geared toward children with learning and behavior issues, offering more direct support for your child without the need for additional services through the public school system.

Homeschool

- Federal law requires school districts to find and evaluate all children with disabilities. This includes homeschooled students. However, how the law is implemented varies from state to state and even from school district to school district.
- Some school districts treat homeschooled students as private school students and may offer a service plan which is similar to an IEP but offers less, or they may offer nothing.
- Some school districts offer upper level classes or extracurricular activities to homeschoolers. If your child has special educational needs that affect the classes enrolled in, you will need to go through the evaluation and IEP process to receive accommodations or services.

The evaluation and IEP process takes months, with a legally defined length of time each step can take. If you plan to enroll your child in public school at any time, start the process at least four to six months before you want your child to start school. The process includes the initial meeting, the evaluation process and the follow up meeting to review the results and set up the IEP and any related services.

You can enroll your child at any time during this process but he will be in a general education classroom with no supports until this final meeting is complete and you have a signed IEP. In general, if your child is not in public school you will be the one who creates a suitable educational plan for your child and makes it happen.

35

Are there any other educational issues related to apraxia of speech?

Apraxia of speech is a neurological disorder that affects:

- Language. Use of language includes hearing, speaking, reading and writing. Early problems with speech and hearing can lead to later problems with reading and writing.
- Motor planning. This includes sequencing. Your child may struggle with sequencing thoughts, numbers, movements for writing or the beginning, middle and end of a story.

One of the most strategic things you can do is to understand how your child learns best and then educate teachers and therapists. You are the expert on your child and you can help teachers and therapists help your child learn when you share what you know.

If apraxia of speech is not your child's only diagnosis, your child will likely need services in other areas besides speech therapy. Schools offer services based on the student's needs. The list of services covers physical, psychological, medical and social needs related to receiving a Free and Appropriate Public Education (FAPE). Some of the most common services students qualify for are:

- Physical therapy (related to accessing the school environment)
- Occupational therapy (related to tasks of daily living)

- Behavioral therapy (related to safety and appropriate behavior in the learning environment)
- Adaptive Physical Education (APE) (program of physical education adapted to a student with disabilities)

36

How will I know my child can read if she can't speak?

Children with apraxia of speech can learn to read even if they cannot speak. You can test individual word knowledge by giving them a choice of three cards with different words, and then asking them to point to a specific word. Make the test more difficult by having two of the words start with the same letter(s).

To test reading comprehension, have them read a sentence or two, then allow them to pick from a set of three pictures which one the story was about. For example, if the sentence is, "The boy went home for dinner," you can show a picture of a house, a store and a school. Or you can show a house with the sun in the morning position, at noon and then sunset for the time of day. Or you can create variations that include two variables.

There are tests designed for this purpose. See if your school or speech therapist will administer these tests to your child. If your child has no speech, make sure the tests are picture based and the results are given in age or grade level equivalents, such as: reading at a first-grade level or third-grade level.

37

What happens after graduation from high school?

The Individuals with Disabilities Education Act (IDEA) is geared toward this moment. The goal of education is to create productive members of society, including people with mild to severe disabilities. If your child is college bound:

- You can get accommodations through *college disability services*. Each college should be able to supply you with a list of the accommodations they offer. Disability services vary widely among higher education programs.
- If your child requires more than the college offers, you can request it from that college or seek a college that offers the accommodations your child needs.
- There are some colleges that specialize in helping students who need above average support and accommodations.
- Some colleges partner with support service organizations to offer help to students who needs extra support. Your child would receive services through the organization instead of the school.

Students with learning disabilities who qualify can stay in the public school system through age 21. This allows extra time for developing job skills and life skills.

- IDEA provides for Transition Planning that must begin at age 14. The last few years of high school are spent developing job skills students can use to work if they are able or life skills to live independently or in a group home setting.
- Once your child graduates, you are often on your own. In the transition out of high school, the schools work with local governmental organizations to train these graduates. There is support for this process but ultimately, your child has to find his or her own job and work to hold the job.
- Communication skills are important for success in adult life. Children with apraxia of speech may take years to develop communication skills, whether speaking or using an AAC device. If your child is not progressing in communication in school, do whatever is necessary to get your school to work on communication skills. That is a battle that needs to be won as early as possible in the school setting.

By graduation, your child should have adopted some form of communication that others can understand. If your child has severe disabilities, this may include a very limited vocabulary but should still be functional. Even merely functional communication can go a long way toward independence.

Section 6

Your Role as Advocate

When you take your newborn baby to the doctor, you are the one who tells the doctor everything about the child and what is going on to get the care he needs. You are functioning as your child's advocate. This same principle applies to your child with apraxia of speech. You will be your child's voice until he develops his own.

The advocacy talked about here is a little more complex than stating facts about your child but it is a skill that can be learned. It is also a service you can hire out. This section explains how advocacy works and how you can learn to advocate for your child.

38

What is an advocate?

An advocate is a person who speaks up for or defends another person's interests, in particular, their legal rights. Professional advocates are experienced in the interests they represent and know the laws and processes behind them.

39

Why does my child need an advocate?

A person with disabilities has certain rights guaranteed by law. The person with disabilities may not be able to understand or communicate at a level to take advantage of or defend those rights. An advocate can help people with disabilities exercise their rights. They may do this within the educational system, the legal system, the medical system or other areas of life governed by disability law.

40

How can I advocate for my child?

As a parent, you qualify as an expert on your child. You can advocate on your child's behalf in any situation from that position of expertise. You may not have a medical or education degree, but you have the equivalent of a degree in your child's life, needs, communication methods, ways of learning new things, ways of expressing pain, developmental progress and so on.

In addition, you will want to become knowledgeable in any area where you feel your child is not getting the care or services she requires or are legally obligated to receive. If your child has a tricky medical problem, research it well so you can discuss it intelligently. You may not know everything about it but you can show that you are informed in the basics. Quote medical studies or opinions to back up what you are requesting. If the problem occurs within the education system, learn your child's rights and bring them to the school's attention. Quote legal cases or laws that back up your claims.

Advocating for your child can take a lot of energy. In the early days, you may not be able to effectively advocate but as you gain experience, you can make a huge difference in your child's care and education. Being an effective advocate requires good listening skills, keeping emotions out of the conversation, knowing your rights and knowing how the system works. You will likely be an advocate for your child for many years so advocacy skills are a good investment of time.

41

Can I hire someone else to be an advocate?

You can advocate for your child at any time. However, there are times when you may need an experienced advocate with the appropriate background who has knowledge of the laws governing your area of need. There are advocacy organizations with different types of advocates. If you are looking for an education advocate, you will need to find one who is familiar with the laws of your state since implementation of educational law is determined by each state. Even better is to find one who is familiar with your county or school district.

Hiring an advocate can be expensive so choose your battles with the school wisely and know exactly what you want to achieve. Educate yourself on what an advocate does. Check for ones with experience related to your situation. An advocate will not make decisions for you but can help you get care and services appropriate to your child's condition.

42

What do I do when it seems everyone is against what I believe my child needs?

You are the expert on your child. No one else has the same interest or level of knowledge about your child that you do. If you cannot find anyone who supports your views, consider why before taking action. Listen carefully to what people say they are against. There may be some nugget(s) of truth they share that you should consider.

Ultimately, it is your responsibility to direct the care of your child. Research the issue in order to make an informed decision on what you think is best for your child. Use facts and data, not emotions or wishful thinking. Your faith may also play a part in what you decide to do. If your child has special needs, you will need the help and wisdom of other people. Gather the best team possible, one that will help you work in your child's best interest.

-

Section 7

Bonus Section: Tips, How To and Encouragement

One of the biggest problems with being a special needs parent is that often, you don't know what you don't know. This section includes things you might want to know but wouldn't necessarily think to ask. These are all things I learned over the course of raising my daughter. The answers to these questions will give you more confidence in dealing with professionals and advocating for your child. Just take one day at a time, one step at a time and things will start to fall into place.

43

How do I evaluate a doctor?

There are many ways to evaluate whether you want to hire a particular doctor, such as:

- How long is the wait time in the office?
- How long does it take to get an appointment?
- How organized is the staff?
- How do you get care if something happens after hours?
- Does the doctor listen to you fully or listen lightly and kind of put your case in a predefined box?
- And, of course, check reviews online.

But how do you find out about a doctor's philosophy of medicine? You could ask the doctor about his views at an appointment but there may not be enough time and sometimes it is difficult to gauge the answers. One of the best ways I've found to evaluate a doctor's approach is to ask the doctor to recommend books or medical studies related to your child's case. This will often tell you a lot about how the doctor views your child's diagnosis. It allows you to see if your understanding of your child's diagnosis and treatment is in line with your doctor's.

44

How do I evaluate a therapist?

When choosing a speech therapist, there are many variables. You will need to prioritize these questions according to your child's needs.

Qualifications

- Does the therapist have at least an MA or MS degree?
- Is the therapist ASHA certified? (AAA after the degree)
- Does the therapist have any additional training or certifications related to treating apraxia of speech such as PROMPT, Kaufman or Speech E-Z? Note: insurance may or may not cover therapy if they consider it experimental and not evidence based so take note of that when filing claims.
- Does the therapist specialize in pediatric clients?
- Does the therapist have experience in your area of need? (CAS, swallowing, stuttering, autism)
- How many children has she treated with CAS (or your area of need)?
- How does her treatment for CAS vary from how she treats other disorders?

Relationships

- Does the therapist seem to like my child?
- Does my child like the therapist? (Different question than: Does my child like to do the hard work of speech therapy? The answer to the latter is probably not, so be sure to separate the two.)
- Is the therapist able to motivate my child to work, even when my child resists?
- Does the therapist have a good reputation among other therapists? Speech therapists are a small community. Most of them know each other so ask questions of other therapists. On a professional level, they probably will not bad-mouth another therapist but you may be able to get a feel for the reputation by how a therapist responds to your questions.

Office Related

- Is the office well organized? Speech therapists have to exhibit a certain amount of organization to do the work of speech therapy so a well-organized office is a good sign.
- What is the cancellation policy?
- Does the therapist take my insurance?
- Is the location convenient for my needs?

Once Therapy has Begun

- Is my child making progress?
- Is the therapist able to explain what she does in ways that I understand?
- Does the therapist give me a mini-update after each session?
- Does the therapist let me observe my child during a session?
- Is the therapist prepared each week for the entire session?

- Does the therapist give me homework so my child is working on speech every day at home, not just 30 minutes a week during a therapy session?
- Does the therapist provide regular written reports of progress? (typically, every three or six months)

45

How do I fire a doctor?

To fire a doctor, you can simply stop making appointments with that particular provider. If you do change doctors:

- Make sure there is continuity of care, meaning have an appointment with the replacement doctor before you cancel any appointments with the first doctor.
- Be sure to get your child's complete medical record from the original doctor's office in anticipation of providing the information to the new doctor. Getting medical records can take weeks or months so plan ahead. It is a good idea to get your child's medical records from his doctors regularly to keep on file at home.
- Once you have everything set up with the new doctor, don't forget to cancel any appointments with the original doctor so you don't get charged as a no-show. Be absolutely certain the appointment is cancelled. Don't just leave a message with an answering service or voicemail.

46

How do I fire a therapist?

Firing a therapist might be more difficult than firing a doctor, even if you have a good relationship with her. With a therapist, your child typically sees her weekly, so both you and your child have developed a relationship with the therapist.

- If you are leaving on good terms, communicate your circumstances to the therapist.
- If you are leaving on less than good terms, you can simply stop making appointments, but it would be better to open the lines of communication if you want to try to make it work for you and your child. (See next question.)
- Be sure to request a final progress report for your child, especially if it has been more than six months since your last report.
- Because therapists are often paid by appointment, they appreciate when you can give them weeks or months of notice so they can fill your child's slot and not suffer a loss of income.
- Also remember that the speech therapist community is small and word gets around. It's best to leave on good terms so you do not become "that parent."

47

What do I do when therapy isn't working?

At times, it may seem that speech therapy is not working. This could be for many reasons. Here is a list of some possibilities and what to do about them.

- Your child may not be neurologically ready for a particular skill. You can: step back a skill level, break the skill into smaller chunks, add neurological supports such as diet changes or additional therapies.
- The therapist may not have experience with the type of therapy needed for your child's situation. You can: see if the therapist is willing to go for training in the therapy your child needs, find a new therapist.
- Your child may be having other problems, diagnosed or undiagnosed, that are getting in the way of progress in speech therapy. You can: research your child's symptoms or problems and see if other families are having similar problems with speech. You can: determine ways to help your child succeed in speech therapy such as behavior therapy, changing the time of day or day of the week, adding supplemental therapies to support overall body function.
- The therapist does not connect well with your child. You can: find a new therapist. There is not really a way to force a connection so it is best to find a therapist with who your child will work with.

48

How do I set up my home to encourage communication?

Children with apraxia of speech will need help with learning language and communication. There are several things you can do to help.

- Fill their world with language by
    - labeling items around the house with the name of the item
    - reading books and pointing to words as you read
    - writing words out as you say them so they are in context of an activity and then review them over time (research Soma Rapid Prompting)
- Since you know you will be doing speech therapy homework, set up a work area with all tools and supplies at hand. Having a consistent place to work helps your child know what to expect and allows you to be ready when it's time to get to work.
- If your child is sensitive to environmental factors, she may be so focused on her reaction to these that she does not have the mental energy to communicate. Evaluate the therapy area, playroom, bedroom and eating area. You don't have to address every one of these but if your child seems agitated or distracted, consider these as possible causes and try to adjust your child's environment:
    - noise level
    - temperature
    - lighting

- o textures
- o colors
- o visible distractions (toys or TV screens in view)
- o time of day
- o physical comfort (hard chair, annoying clothing)
- Watch *Signing Time*® videos so your child can begin communicating in a no tech way. You can purchase the videos, borrow them from the library or get a monthly subscription with access to all the beginner videos.
- Include language-based toys among her regular toys.
- Add a mirror to the play area so she can see herself talk.
- Hang a swing or hammock indoors or outdoors accessible to your child. The sensory input from a swing really helps some children.
- Play classical music in the background. There is no specific music center in the brain so music affects the whole brain. The complex interplay of instruments in classical music lights up different parts of the brain, as shown in brain scans.
- Warning: some types of music or musical instruments may cause your child to react negatively. Some examples are:
  - o Fugues or any music played in a minor key
  - o Violins, which can sound rather screechy
  - o High-pitched woodwinds like piccolos, flutes and oboes
  - o Guitars, when played a certain way
  - o Percussion such as drums, cymbals and cow bells

49

How important is speech therapy homework?

In general, children with apraxia of speech will not learn how to talk on their own. They need therapy to teach their mouths to cooperate with their brains (see answer to question 1). They need the process of speech broken into pieces that they can practice and eventually put them all together.

Practice is the key and that is where speech therapy homework comes in. Expect to spend time every day intentionally working on speech therapy homework. Doing speech homework accomplishes several things:

- You are spending time with your child in a meaningful activity. Quality time can be hard to achieve with a child who does not speak. Make the most of these guided activities as opportunities for relationship building.
- You are helping to lay the foundation for communication as your child interacts with you.
- Each time you work with your child you are helping his brain with speech. The progress may be miniscule but each victory is a step toward communication.
- You are learning skills you can apply throughout the years your child needs speech therapy. As your child grows older you may find it more difficult to get adequate speech therapy services through the school. You will have to pay for private therapy or

work on speech at home with homework from the school therapist. Any skills developed up to this point will be helpful.

- You will know how your child learns and can share that with
  teachers and therapists, saving them hours of trial and error.

50

Are there any tips for interpreting standardized test results?

Standardized tests are based on norms, meaning what is considered "normal" for a child by a certain age. If your child is significantly behind, you may get a result like: >.1%. That number indicates that for a child of the same grade level, your child's scores measure less than .1% of all children who took that test nationwide during that semester. If your child's problems are significant, this number is meaningless as each time your child is evaluated, that number will likely stay the same. For children to qualify for special education, the school has to use these normed tests to prove that they are behind their peers.

The good news is that standardized test results can be converted to age or grade level equivalents, which is much more helpful and meaningful. Let's say that a result of >.1% in fourth grade converted might show that your child is actually performing at a 6 years 3 months level, which is first grade. When tested again three years later, the same >.1% converted shows your child is now performing at an 8-year 6-month level, which is mid-third grade. This would show that your child made 2 years 3 months of progress in those three years. In order to make this comparison, the child must be given the same brand of test for consecutive evaluations, for example the Woodcock-Johnson or the Wechsler Intelligence Scale for Children (WISC-IV).

Be sure to request all standardized test results in age equivalents at the time the test is given. If you request it at the time the test is given for a school-provided evaluation, make sure you have those age equivalents at the IEP meeting so you can discuss them.

Most, if not all, standardized tests that are normed can be converted to age equivalents including standardized reading tests given in the classroom, not just those administered for the three-year evaluations required to qualify for an IEP.

51

How do I advocate for my child in other environments (family, church, public places)?

Advocating for your child is an important part of your job as parent. Advocating requires a combination of educating others on what your child needs and fighting for legal rights for your child when necessary. In a lot of places, your role will simply be to educate those around you about your child: how they learn, how they communicate, their abilities and so on.

Every person with disabilities has legally protected rights. At times, you will need to remind people about these rights and see that they are protected. Become familiar with both the education rights and civil rights of persons with disabilities so you can help others uphold your child's rights. If a legal issue arises, you can work with a professional advocate or hire an attorney to help you resolve the issue.

52

Should I set up a temporary guardian?

A temporary guardian is someone you legally designate to take your child in a case where the legal guardians (usually parents) are not able to take care of the child. No one really wants to think about this but accidents do happen and with a child who does not communicate well, this is one thing you can do proactively to help your child.

For example, if you and your spouse were in a car accident and had children in the vehicle, who would take care of the children? If the answer is not clear for whatever reason, the children may be put into the foster care system temporarily until things can be sorted out.

You can help avoid this situation by legally declaring temporary guardians who will receive your child into their home. Once you have set this up through an attorney, keep a card in your wallet with the names of these guardians in the order of contact, with your first choice listed first. With children who cannot communicate well, it is important to place them with someone who knows them and how they communicate, especially in unexpected circumstances like these. This can keep your child in a safe and familiar environment until the situation is resolved.

53

What should I know about urgent care and emergency room visits?

Be aware that your insurance company may require prior authorization for urgent care and emergency room visits. If your child has feeding or swallowing problems related to speech or has health issues that might require emergency care, it is a good idea to look up these requirements in advance so you know the procedure. In the case of a life or death emergency, seek immediate care. Then call your insurance company as soon as you can to sort it out.

You should also be aware that even though a hospital is in-network, the doctors and specialists who practice there might not be in your insurance company's network of providers. This can make for a nasty surprise when you see your hospital bill and you have charges for out-of-network practitioners. If you expect a lot of emergency room visits, you may be able to work with your insurance company to identify the in-network providers and use them whenever possible.

54

What are your top resources for speech concerns?

The resources listed below are managed by groups rather than an individual. Using these as a starting point will help you get the big picture. As you learn more about your child's diagnosis, you can search for websites run by individuals that are specific to your child's needs.

WrightsLaw.com – Extensive legal information related to IDEA and its implementation.

Understood.org – Cooperative effort of 15 nonprofit organizations to provide information and support for parents of children with intellectual and learning disabilities.

Apraxia-Kids.org – A nonprofit organization committed to educating parents and professionals and raise awareness in the community. They offer articles, webinars and a national conference, among other things.

ASHA.org – Extensive library of research-based information related to speech and hearing including childhood apraxia of speech (CAS). The schools are accustomed to using only or mostly research-based methods so using ASHA's reports and studies as supporting documentation will be helpful for building a case for your child's services.

55

Where do I go from here?

This book contains a lot of information representing huge areas of your life. The good news is, you won't need it all at the same time. Take a look at the sections in this book. Figure out which one represents your most urgent need and start there. This book is borne out of my own experiences and lots of research in each of these areas. I'm willing to help you gain your footing. If you need a little hand-holding to figure out what to do next, please join me at ArtofSpecialNeedsParenting.com where I help parents teach their kids independence, social connection and productivity.

Stephanie Buckwalter

FROM THE AUTHOR:

Thank you for purchasing this book. My greatest wish is to help other parents bust through the learning curve for dealing with the system, whether medical or educational. I appreciate the trust you have placed in me by reading this book.

- If the material was helpful, please leave a review and let others know how it helped you.
- If you have comments or unanswered questions, please contact me at ArtofSpecialNeedsParenting.com. I am interested in hearing from both parents and SLPs.
- If you struggle in any area of special needs parenting, you can request a *Guide To* book for those topics. Please submit your request on my website.

45653831R00063